Need For Speed
CARS

LEO MARRIOTT

Published in 2009 by TAJ Books International LLP

27, Ferndown Gardens,
Cobham,
Surrey,
UK,
KT11 2BH

www.tajbooks.com

ISBN-13: 978-1-84406-136-5

Printed in China.

Need For Speed
CARS

LEO MARRIOTT

T&J

INTRODUCTION

Although Nicolas-Joseph Cugnot is often credited with building the first self-propelled mechanical vehicle or automobile in about 1769, this claim is disputed by some, who doubt Cugnot's three-wheeler ever ran. Others claim Ferdinand Verbiest, a member of a Jesuit mission in China, built the first steam-powered 'car' around 1672. What is not in doubt is that Richard Trevithick built and demonstrated his Puffing Devil road locomotive in 1801, the first truly successful steam-powered road vehicle.

François Isaac de Rivaz, a Swiss inventor, designed the first internal combustion engine, in 1806, which was fuelled by a mixture of hydrogen and oxygen and used it to develop the world's first vehicle to run on such an engine. The design was not very successful, as was the case with Samuel Brown, Samuel Morey, and Etienne Lenoir who each produced vehicles powered by clumsy internal combustion engines.

In November 1881 French inventor Gustave Trouvé demonstrated a working three-wheeled automobile. This was at the International Exhibition of Electricity in Paris.

An automobile powered by an Otto gasoline engine was built in Mannheim, Germany by Karl Benz in 1885 and granted a patent in January of the following year under the auspices of his major company, Benz & Cie. which was founded in 1883.

Although several other German engineers (including Gottlieb Daimler, Wilhelm Maybach, and Siegfried Marcus) were working on the problem at about the same time, Karl Benz is generally acknowledged as the inventor of the modern automobile. In 1879 Benz was granted a patent for his first engine, designed in 1878. Many of his other inventions made the use of the internal combustion engine feasible for powering a vehicle and in 1896, Benz designed and patented the first internal combustion flat engine.

Approximately 25 Benz vehicles were built and sold before 1893, when his first four-wheeler was introduced. They were powered with four-stroke engines of his own design. Emile Roger of France, already producing Benz engines under license, now added the Benz automobile to his line of products. Because France was more open to the early automobiles, more were built and sold in France through Roger than Benz sold in Germany.

Daimler and Maybach founded Daimler Motoren Gesellschaft (Daimler Motor Company, DMG) in Cannstatt in 1890 and under the brand name, Daimler, sold their first automobile in 1892. By 1895 about 30 vehicles had been built by Daimler and Maybach, either at the Daimler works or in the Hotel Hermann, where they set up shop after falling out with their backers. Benz and Daimler seem to have been unaware of each other's early work and worked independently. Daimler died in 1900 and later that year, Maybach designed a model named Daimler-Mercedes, special-ordered by Emil Jellinek. Two years later, a new model DMG automobile was produced and named Mercedes after the engine. Maybach quit DMG shortly thereafter and opened a business of his own. Rights to the Daimler brand name were sold to other manufacturers.

Karl Benz proposed co-operation between DMG and Benz & Cie. when economic conditions began to deteriorate in Germany following the First World War, but the directors of DMG refused to consider it initially. Negotiations between the two companies resumed several years later and in 1924 they signed an Agreement of Mutual Interest valid until the year 2000. Both enterprises standardized design, production, purchasing, sales, and advertising—marketing their automobile models jointly—although keeping their respective brands. On June 28, 1926, Benz & Cie. and DMG finally merged as the Daimler-Benz company, baptizing all of its automobiles Mercedes Benz honoring the most important model of the DMG automobiles, the Maybach design later referred to as the 1902 Mercedes-35hp, along with the Benz name. Karl Benz remained a member of the board of directors of Daimler-Benz until his death in 1929.

In 1890, Emile Levassor and Armand Peugeot of France began producing vehicles with Daimler engines, and so laid the foundation of the motor industry in France. The first American car with a gasoline internal combustion engine supposedly was designed in 1877 by George Selden of Rochester, New York, who applied for a patent on an automobile in 1879. In Britain there had been several attempts to build steam cars with varying degrees of success with Thomas Rickett even attempting a production run in 1860. Santler from Malvern is recognized by the Veteran Car Club of Great Britain as having made the first petrol-powered car in the country in 1894 followed by Frederick William Lanchester in 1895 but these were both one-offs. The first production vehicles came from the Daimler Motor Company, founded by Harry J. Lawson in 1896, and making their first cars in 1897.

In 1892, German engineer Rudolf Diesel got a patent for a "New Rational Combustion Engine". In 1897 he built the first Diesel Engine. In 1895, Selden was granted a United States patent (U.S. Patent 549,160) for a two-stroke automobile engine, which hindered more than encouraged development of autos in the United States. Steam, electric, and gasoline powered autos competed for decades, with gasoline internal combustion engines achieving dominance in the 1910s.

Although various pistonless rotary engine designs have attempted to compete with the conventional piston and crankshaft design, only Mazda's version of the Wankel engine has had more than very limited success.

Production

The large-scale, production-line manufacturing of affordable automobiles was debuted by Ransom Olds at his Oldsmobile factory in 1902. This concept was then greatly expanded by Henry Ford, beginning in 1914.

As a result, Ford's cars came off the line in fifteen minute intervals, much faster than previous methods, increasing production by seven to one (requiring 12.5 man-hours before, 1 hour 33 minutes after), while using less manpower. It was so successful, paint became a bottleneck. Only Japan black would dry fast enough, forcing the company to drop the variety of colors available before 1914, until fast-drying Duco lacquer was developed in 1926. In 1914, an assembly line worker could buy a Model T with four months' pay.

Ford's complex safety procedures—especially assigning each worker to a specific location instead of allowing them to roam about—dramatically reduced the rate of injury. The combination of high wages and high efficiency is called "Fordism," and was copied by most major industries. The efficiency gains from the assembly line also coincided with the take off of the United States. The assembly line forced workers to work at a certain pace with very repetitive motions which led to more output per worker while other countries were using less productive methods.

In the automotive industry, its success was dominating, and quickly spread worldwide. Ford France and Ford Britain in 1911, Ford Denmark 1923, Ford Germany 1925; in 1921, Citroen was the first native European manufacturer to adopt it. Soon, companies had to have assembly lines, or risk going broke; by 1930, 250 companies which did not had disappeared.

Development of automotive technology was rapid, due in part to the hundreds of small manufacturers competing to gain the world's attention. Key developments included electric ignition and the electric self-starter (both by Charles Kettering, for the Cadillac Motor Company in 1910-1911), independent suspension, and four-wheel brakes.

Since the 1920s, nearly all cars have been mass-produced to meet market needs, so marketing plans have often heavily influenced automobile design. It was Alfred P. Sloan who established the idea of different makes of cars produced by one company, so buyers could "move up" as their fortunes improved.

Reflecting the rapid pace of change, makes shared parts with one another so larger production volume resulted in lower costs for each price range. For example, in the 1930s, LaSalles, sold by Cadillac, used cheaper mechanical parts made by Oldsmobile; in the 1950s, Chevrolet shared hood, doors, roof, and windows with Pontiac; by the 1990s, corporate drivetrains and shared platforms (with interchangeable brakes, suspension, and other parts) were common. Even so, only major makers could afford high costs, and even companies with decades of production, such as Apperson, Cole, Dorris, Haynes, or Premier, could not manage: of some two hundred carmakers in existence in 1920, only 43 survived in 1930, and with the Great Depression, by 1940, only 17 of those were left.

In Europe, much the same would happen. Morris set up its production line at Cowley in 1924, and soon outsold Ford, while beginning in 1923 to follow Ford's practise of vertical integration, buying Hotchkiss (engines), Wrigley (gearboxes), and Osberton (radiators), for instance, as well as competitors, such as Wolseley: in 1925, Morris had 41% of total British car production. Most British small-car assemblers, from Autocrat to Meteorite to Seabrook, to name only three, had gone under. Germany's first mass-manufactured car, the Opel 4PS Laubfrosch (Tree Frog), came off the line at Russelsheim in 1924, soon making Opel the top car builder in Germany, with 37.5% of the market.

Most automobiles in use today are propelled by gasoline (also known as petrol) or diesel internal combustion engines, which are known to cause air pollution and are also blamed for contributing to climate change and global warming. Increasing costs of oil-based fuels, tightening environmental laws and restrictions on greenhouse gas emissions are propelling work on alternative power systems for automobiles. Efforts to improve or replace existing technologies include the development of hybrid vehicles, and electric and hydrogen vehicles which do not release pollution into the air.

A Classic 1930's Maybach Zeppelin

Ransom E. Olds as a passenger

Diesel

Diesel-engined cars have long been popular in Europe with the first models being introduced in the 1930s by Mercedes Benz and Citroen. The main benefit of diesel engines is a 50% fuel burn efficiency compared with 27% in the best gasoline engines. A down-side of the diesel is the presence in the exhaust gases of fine soot particulates and manufacturers are now starting to fit filters to remove these. Many diesel-powered cars can also run with little or no modifications on 100% biodiesel.

Gasoline

Gasoline engines have the advantage over diesel in being lighter and able to work at higher rotational speeds and they are the usual choice for fitting in high-performance sports cars. Continuous development of gasoline engines for over a hundred years has produced improvements in efficiency and reduced pollution. The carburetor was used on nearly all road car engines until the 1980s but it was long realised better control of the fuel/air mixture could be achieved with fuel injection. Indirect fuel injection was first used in aircraft engines from 1909, in racing car engines from the 1930s, and road cars from the late 1950s. Gasoline Direct Injection (GDI) is now starting to appear in production vehicles such as the 2007 (Mark II) BMW Mini. Exhaust gases are also cleaned up by fitting a catalytic converter into the exhaust system. Clean air legislation in many of the car industries most important markets has made both catalysts and fuel injection virtually universal fittings. Most modern gasoline engines are also capable of running with up to 15% ethanol mixed into the gasoline - older vehicles may have seals and hoses that can be harmed by ethanol. With a small amount of redesign, gasoline-powered vehicles can run on ethanol concentrations as high as 85%. 100% ethanol is used in some parts of the world (such as Brazil), but vehicles must be started on pure gasoline and switched over to ethanol once the engine is running. Most gasoline engined cars can also run on LPG with the addition of an LPG tank for fuel storage and carburetion modifications to add an LPG mixer. LPG produces fewer toxic emissions and Is a popular fuel for fork lift trucks that have to operate inside buildings.

Bioalcohols and biogasoline

Ethanol, other alcohol fuels (biobutanol) and biogasoline have widespread use an automotive fuel. Most alcohols have less energy per liter than gasoline and are usually blended with gasoline. Alcohols are used for a variety of reasons - to increase octane, to improve emissions, and as an alternative to petroleum based fuel, since they can be made from agricultural crops. Brazil's ethanol program provides about 20% of the nations automotive fuel needs, including several million cars that operate on pure ethanol.

Electric

The first electric cars were built around 1832, well before internal combustion powered cars appeared. For a period of time electrics were considered superior due to the silent nature of electric motors compared to the very loud noise of the gasoline engine. This advantage was removed with Hiram Percy Maxim's invention of the muffler in 1897. Thereafter internal combustion powered cars had two critical advantages: 1) long range and 2) high specific energy (far lower weight of petrol fuel versus weight of batteries). The building of battery electric vehicles that could rival internal combustion models had to wait for the introduction of modern semiconductor controls and improved batteries. Because they can deliver a high torque at low revolutions electric cars do not require such a complex drive train and transmission as internal combustion powered cars. Some post-2000 electric car designs such as the Venturi Fétish are able to accelerate from 0-60 mph (96 km/h) in 4.0 seconds with a top speed around 130 mph (210 km/h). Others have a range of 250 miles (400 km) on the EPA highway cycle requiring 3-1/2 hours to completely charge. Equivalent fuel efficiency to internal combustion is not well defined but some press reports give it at around 135 mpg–U.S. (1.74 L/100 km / 162.1 mpg–imp).

Steam

Steam power, usually using an oil or gas heated boiler, was also in use until the 1930s but had the major disadvantage of being unable to power the car until boiler pressure was available. It has the advantage of being able to produce very low emissions as the combustion process can be carefully controlled. Its disadvantages include poor heat efficiency and extensive requirements for electric auxiliaries.

Gas turbine

In the 1950s there was a brief interest in using gas turbine (jet) engines and several makers including Rover and Chrysler produced include the development of hybrid vehicles, and electric and hydrogen vehicles which do not release pollution into the air.

Diesel

Diesel-engined cars have long been popular in Europe with the first models being introduced in the 1930s by Mercedes Benz and Citroen. The main benefit of diesel engines is a 50% fuel burn efficiency compared with 27% in the best gasoline engines. A down-side of the diesel is the presence in the exhaust gases of fine soot particulates and manufacturers are now starting to fit filters to remove these. Many diesel-powered cars can also run with little or no modifications on 100% biodiesel.

Gasoline

Gasoline engines have the advantage over diesel in being lighter and able to work at higher rotational speeds and they are the usual choice for fitting in high-performance sports cars. Continuous development of gasoline engines for over a hundred years has produced improvements in efficiency and reduced pollution. The carburetor was used on nearly all road car engines until the 1980s but it was long realised better control of the fuel/air mixture could be achieved with fuel injection. Indirect fuel injection was first used in aircraft engines from 1909, in racing car engines from the 1930s, and road cars from the late 1950s. Gasoline Direct Injection (GDI) is now starting to appear in production vehicles such as the 2007 (Mark II) BMW Mini. Exhaust gases are also cleaned up by fitting a catalytic converter into the exhaust system. Clean air legislation in many of the car industries most important markets has made both catalysts and fuel injection virtually universal fittings. Most modern gasoline engines are also capable of running with up to 15% ethanol mixed into the gasoline - older vehicles may have seals and hoses that can be harmed by ethanol. With a small amount of redesign, gasoline-powered vehicles can run on ethanol concentrations as high as 85%. 100% ethanol is used in some parts of the world (such as Brazil), but vehicles must be started on pure gasoline and switched over to ethanol once the engine is running. Most gasoline engined cars can also run on LPG with the addition of an LPG tank for fuel storage and carburetion modifications to add an LPG mixer. LPG produces fewer toxic emissions and is a popular fuel for fork lift trucks that have to operate inside buildings.

Bioalcohols and biogasoline

Ethanol, other alcohol fuels (biobutanol) and biogasoline have widespread use an automotive fuel. Most alcohols have less energy per liter than gasoline and are usually blended with gasoline. Alcohols are used for a variety of reasons - to increase octane, to improve emissions, and as an alternative to petroleum based fuel, since they can be made from agricultural crops. Brazil's ethanol program provides about 20% of the nations automotive fuel needs, including several million cars that operate on pure ethanol.

Electric

The first electric cars were built around 1832, well before internal combustion powered cars appeared. For a period of time electrics were considered superior due to the silent nature of electric motors compared to the very loud noise of the gasoline engine. This advantage was removed with Hiram Percy Maxim's invention of the muffler in 1897. Thereafter internal combustion powered cars had two critical advantages: 1) long range and 2) high specific energy (far lower weight of petrol fuel versus weight of batteries). The building of battery electric vehicles that could rival internal combustion models had to wait for the introduction of modern semiconductor controls and improved batteries. Because they can deliver a high torque at low revolutions electric cars do not require such a complex drive train and transmission as internal combustion powered cars. Some post-2000 electric car designs such as the Venturi Fétish are able to accelerate from 0-60 mph (96 km/h) in 4.0 seconds with a top speed around 130 mph (210 km/h). Others have a range of 250 miles (400 km) on the EPA highway cycle requiring 3-1/2 hours to completely charge. Equivalent fuel efficiency to internal combustion is not well defined but some press reports give it at around 135 mpg–U.S. (1.74 L/100 km / 162.1 mpg–imp).

Steam

Steam power, usually using an oil or gas heated boiler, was also in use until the 1930s but had the major disadvantage of being unable to power the car until boiler pressure was available. It has the advantage of being able to produce very low emissions as the combustion process can be carefully controlled. Its disadvantages include poor heat efficiency and extensive requirements for electric auxiliaries.

Toyota Prius, the top selling hybrid worldwide.

ALFA ROMEO 159

The Alfa Romeo 159 is a compact executive car produced by the Italian manufacturer Alfa Romeo. Designed by Giorgetto Giugiaro in collaboration with the Alfa Centro Stile. The nose features a traditional Alfa Romeo V-shaped grille and bonnet, and cylindrical head light clusters. A high waistline broadens until it reaches the rear "C" pillar. The interior also features styling treatments familiar from earlier cars, including the 156, such as deeply recessed instruments which are angled towards the driver. The 159 is available in both front and four-wheel drive configurations. The "Q4" four-wheel drive system utilises a Torsen type C twin differential (front and center differential in the same unit) and is available on the 3.2 litre petrol and 2.4 litre diesel engines. The gearbox is a six-speed manual on most models (1.8 has a five-speed), and a six-speed automatic Q-Tronic gearbox (Aisin AW TF-80SC) is available for the 1.9 diesel, 2.4 diesel and 3.2 petrol models. The Selespeed gearbox is for sale in some countries with the 2.2 petrol engine. A Sportwagon variant of the 159 was introduced at the Geneva Motor Show in 2006. An automatic gearbox option for the 2.4 JTDM diesel model was also launched that year, and later extended to other versions. In 2007 a four wheel drive diesel model was released and the 2.4-litre diesel engines' power output increased to 210 PS (207 hp/154 kW), with a newly reintroduced TI trim level also available as an option. For the 2009 model year, Alfa Romeo is introducing a new turbocharged petrol engine badged as "TBi". This 1742 cc unit has direct injection and variable valve timing in both inlet and exhaust cams. This new engine has 200 PS (147 kW; 197 hp) and 320 N·m (240 lb·ft) of torque. Eventually this unit will replace GM derived 2.2 and 1.9 JTS units. Also a new 170 PS (125 kW; 168 hp) JTDm diesel will become available.

ALFA ROMEO 8C COMPETIZIONE

During the Mondial de l'Automobile 2006, Alfa Romeo announced the production of a limited series of 500 units of the 8C Competizione. The production version is very similar to the concept, with the biggest difference to the exterior being the rear-hinged hood. The car came in four colours: 8C Red, Competition Red, black or yellow. The bodyshell is made of carbon fibre, produced by ATR Group. The carbon fibre body is fitted to a steel chassis, made by Italian company ITCA Produzione. The final assembly takes place at the Maserati factory in Modena, Italy. The car uses a modified Maserati platform and powertrain (Maserati 4200, GranTurismo) and features a Ferrari/Maserati derived 90 degree cross-plane dry-sump lubricated 4.7-litre V8 assembled by Ferrari. The top engine performance figures may be summarized as a maximum power of 331 kilowatts (450 PS) at 7000 revolutions per minute, a peak torque of 480 newton metres (354 lbf·ft) at 4750 rpm (80% at 2500 rpm) with an engine redline of 7500 rpm and rev limiter of 7600 rpm. The V8 engine has variable timing in intake valves and compression ratio of 11.3.TThe gearbox can shift in 175 milliseconds when using Sport mode. The 8C also has a limited slip differential. It is fitted with specially developed 20 inch tyres: 245/35 at the front and 285/35 at the rear, fitted on perforated rims in fluid moulded aluminium. The 8C brakes have been called "phenomenal" by Road & Track magazine, with a stopping distance of 32 metres (105.0 ft), when travelling at an initial speed of 97 kilometres per hour (60 mph). The official top speed is announced to be 292 kilometres per hour (181 mph) but it might be higher, with estimations that it could be around 306 kilometres per hour (190 mph) according to the Road & Track magazine.

ASTON MARTIN DBS

The Aston Martin DBS is a GT car produced by the British manufacturer Aston Martin Lagonda Limited. Originally produced from 1967-72, it featured in the 1969 James Bond film On Her Majesty's Secret Service. A new version, based heavily on the Aston Martin DB9, is featured in the 2006 film Casino Royale and the 2008 film Quantum of Solace

The new DBS is based on the DB9, more specifically the DBR9 race car. Built on the VH Platform the car shares its roof, sidescreens and wheelbase with the DB9, but sits lower (by 25 mm) and wider (by 40 mm) than the DB9. Visually, the front end is dominated by air scoops and cooling ducts which help cool the six-litre V12 engine which has reportedly been uprated to produce 510 bhp (380 kW; 517 PS) , 420 lb·ft (569 N·m) of torque & a top speed of 191 mph (307 km/h). At the rear are a carbon diffuser and an integrated rear lip spoiler. Other details include a six-speed manual transmission and a removable stopwatch. A special helmet pod behind the driver's seat is present for Casino Royale but will not feature in the production version. The Aston Martin DBS also features an optional Bang & Olufsen sound system with 13 active loudspeakers including 2 tweeters with ALT (Acoustic Lens Technology)[3]. Aston Martin is expected to build only 300 examples of the new DBS

ASTON MARTIN ONE77

The Aston Martin One-77 is a sports car by Aston Martin. It first appeared at the 2008 Paris Motor Show, although the car remained mostly covered by a "Savile Row tailored skirt" throughout the show. The One-77 will feature a full carbon fibre monocoque chassis, a handcrafted aluminium body, and a 7.3 litre V12 engine with over 700 hp (520 kW). It will have a limited run of 77 units with delivery starting in October 2009.

Prior to the One-77's Paris Motor Show debut, the website 925.nl had leaked various details about the car. In addition to the now official information listed above, the article revealed the One-77 will cost approximately £1,050,000. The engine will be naturally aspirated, and the car will have a 6-speed automated manual transmission, height-adjustable suspension, dynamic stability control and carbon-ceramic brakes.

According to the Australian newspaper, The Courier-Mail, the car is expected to be priced at around AU$2.6 million. Also the British magazine, Top Gear, noted that it is to be priced at £1,200,000.

At the 2009 Geneva Auto Show, the company revealed the car fully. It features Pirelli P Zero Corsa tyres (255/35 ZR20 front, 335/30 ZR20 rear), 6-speed transmission, Carbon Ceramic Matrix brake. Top speed was estimated over 200 mph (320 km/h), with a 0-60 mph time in approximately 3.5 seconds. The projected weight was 1,500 kg (3,307 lb).

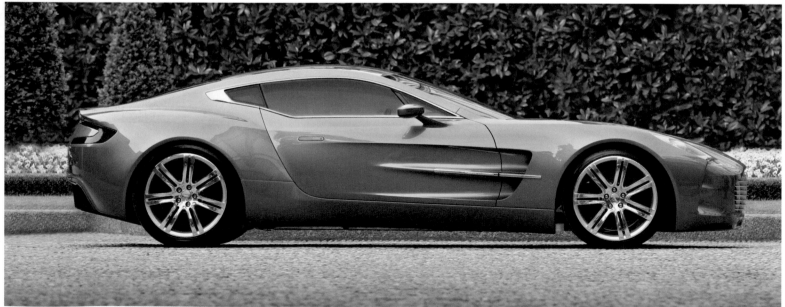

AUDI A5

The Audi A5 is essentially the two-door coupé and cabriolet versions of the fourth generation A4 (B8) saloon and Avant. Audi bills the model as a grand tourer, to compete against the likes of the BMW E92 and the Mercedes-Benz CLK-Class. Audi decided to spin off the cabriolet and new coupé into a nameplate of its own as the A5; otherwise the A5 is essentially the two-door variant of the A4. The new A5 and B8 A4 debuted on the new Audi MLP platform (Modular Longitudinal Platform) which is planned to underpin the next generation A6 and A8. The platform is notable for its departure from Audi's trademark "overhung" engine mounting position over the front axle, in favour of the powertrain being located behind the front axle - in an effort to achieve a more even weight distribution (52:48) between the front and rear wheels. The A5 has adopted many design elements of the Nuvolari quattro concept. The A5 debuted with the 3.2-litre FSI V6 engine delivering 265 PS (261 hp/195 kW). In 2009, Audi announced the S-tronic transmission option for A5 with 2.0L TFSI quattro in UK market. The Audi S5 was released to the public at the same time as the A5. Its heart is a 4.2 L Fuel Stratified Injection (FSI) V8 engine, producing 354 PS (260 kW; 349 hp) at 6800 rpm and 440 N·m (325 lb·ft) at 3,500 rpm. The S5 Cabriolet will receive instead a supercharged 3.0 L V6 TFSI petrol engine. The Audi S5 features a more aggressive fascia (as do most Audi S and RS models), including a string of LED daytime running lights around the bi-Xenon headlamps (although these are available as part of the S-line package on the standard A5). The Audi S5 also comes standard with larger 19" alloy wheels (with different design), bigger brakes, heated leather sport seats, and other convenience features, some of which are available as an option on the standard A5.

AUDI R8

The R8 is based on the Audi Space Frame, which contributes to the car's relatively light weight. Audi announced in 2005 that the name of the successful Audi R8 race car would be used for a new road car in 2007, The Audi R8 is equipped with a 4.2 litre Fuel Stratified Injection (FSI) V8 engine developing 420 PS (309 kW; 414 hp) and 430 N·m (320 ft·lbf), and is basically the same engine used in the B7 Audi RS4, but modified to use dry sump lubrication. A new additional variant with a 5.2 litre Fuel Stratified Injection (FSI) V10 engine was added on the 9th of December 2008, which produces 386 kW (525 PS; 518 hp) and 530 N·m (390 ft·lbf). The transmission is either a manual gearbox with metal gate for the shift lever, or an "R-tronic" gearbox (single-clutch semi-automatic sequential manual transmission). These options are the same as those available on the Lamborghini Gallardo. A double-clutch gearbox (Direct-Shift Gearbox - DSG, now badged by Audi as "S-tronic") is not available. The R8 has a dry weight of 1560 kg (3439 lb). Its suspension uses magneto rheological dampers. As Audi AG owns Lamborghini (Automobili Lamborghini S.p.A.), much of the R8 is shared with the Lamborghini Gallardo, including the transmission. The R8 is made distinct by its exterior styling, cabin, engine, and pricing. Safety features include Bosch ESP 8.0 Electronic Stability Programme with ABS, front dual-stage airbags, and side-impact airbags.

Amongst the options list for the Audi R8 are a Bang & Olufsen sound system, and "Audi Ceramic" Carbon fibre-reinforced Silicon Carbide (C/SiC) composite brakes with monobloc alloy Brembo calipers on all four wheels (6-piston at front, 4-piston at rear) with SGL Carbon ceramic discs.

BENTLEY BROOKLANDS

The Bentley Brooklands is a full-size luxury car introduced for 1992 as a replacement for the Bentley Mulsanne and Bentley Eight models. It was intended as a slightly cheaper alternative to the Bentley Turbo R, featuring the same styling, underpinnings and the Rolls-Royce 6.75-litre engine, but without the more powerful model's turbocharger.

The Brooklands was replaced by the Bentley Arnage in 1998. At the 2007 Geneva Auto Show, Bentley resurrected the Brooklands nameplate for a two-door, four-seat coupé to be built for the 2008 model year.

The Bentley Brooklands Coupé will be hand-assembled, employing traditional coach-building techniques and craftsmanship skills in wood veneer and leather hide. Lifetime production is planned for 550 cars, with deliveries expected to start in the first half of 2008.

The Brooklands is powered by a twin-turbocharged 6 -litre V8 engine producing 530 bhp (395 kW) and 1050 Nm (774 ft·lbf), the highest torque ever developed by a production V8 engine. It can achieve 0-60 mph in around 5 seconds, and a top speed in the region of 296 km/h (184 mph). With an optional Carbon fibre-reinforced Silicon Carbide (C/SiC) cermaic composite braking system with 14inch SGL Carbon brake discs, the new Brooklands offers more stopping power than any passenger vehicle currently available for purchase.

BENTLEY CONTINENTAL GTC SPEED

The Bentley Continental GT is a two-door 2+2 grand touring coupé released in 2003, replacing the previous Rolls-Royce-based Continental R and T. **It is equipped with a** 6.0 litre, twin-turbocharged W12 engine, producing 552 hp (412 kW), with a top speed of 198 mph (319 km/h).

Designed by Belgian stylist Dirk van Braeckel, the Continental GT is built on the Volkswagen Group D1s platform, and therefore shares many technical components with the Volkswagen Phaeton.

The convertible version of the Continental GT, the Continental GTC, was first presented in September 2005, and was introduced to several world markets in the autumn of 2006. With the second generation Azure, it is the second Bentley convertible released in 2005. The roof is produced by Karmann in Osnabrück, Germany.

On 1 August 2007, Bentley released details of a more powerful GT. Power is increased to 603 bhp/449kW (610 PS), with a top speed of 202 miles per hour (325 km/h) and a 0-60 mph time of 4.3 seconds. The Continental's weight is also reduced by 35 kg (77 lb). Minor exterior changes include a tinted front grille and larger exhaust pipes. The price for this model is £137,000. The Continental GT Speed is the first production Bentley officially capable of reaching 202 mph Set to be released in 2009. It will incorporate the same engine as the GT Speed and the Flying Spur Speed.

BMW 6 SERIES

BMW 6 Series refers to two generations of automobile from BMW, both being based on their contemporary 5 Series sedans. The first was the E24, launched in 1976 to replace the 3.0CS & 3.0CSi (E9). In 2003, BMW released the all new E63/E64 which was available as a coupé and convertible. Models were the 645ci (later replaced with the 650i) and the 630i. The highest performance 6 series is the BMW M6.

Competitors include the Cadillac XLR, Mercedes-Benz SL, Lexus SC430, and Jaguar XK.

An all-new 6-Series (E63) was introduced in 2003, filling the hole in the lineup left since the end of the 8-Series' production. Based on the underpinnings of the E60, the new 6-Series was introduced with a 4.4 L 333 PS (245 kW) V8 engine for the 645Ci. In 2004, a more affordable inline six-cylinder engine was introduced in the 630i. This was soon followed by a convertible model (the E64), the first 6-Series with a removable top. Soon after its introduction, the 645Ci was replaced by the 650i, with a larger displacement (4.8 L) and 367 PS (270 kW). The range-topping M6 arrived in late 2005, using the same V10 engine as the M5, with 507 PS (373 kW). In 2007 the 635d (Twin Turbo 3.0L Diesel) was introduced with 286 PS (210 kW) and 430 ft·lbf (580 N·m) which comprehensively outguns the 630i with the added bonus of 41mpg, the 635d Convertible (released shortly afterwards) was described by Autocar as "the best 6-series of the lot."

BMW Z4

The second-generation Z4 was first shown at the 2009 North American International Auto Show in Detroit. The car has a retractable hardtop. The new Z4 replaces the previous roadster and coupé versions for the 2009 model year. The top is made of a two-piece lightweight aluminum shell, and takes 20 seconds to fold up or down. Manufacturing has been moved from the United States to Regensburg, Germany. Three trim levels will be made available in the form of the sDrive23i, sDrive30i, and sDrive35i. The U.S. market will not receive the sDrive23i. The sDrive23i is powered by BMW's 2,497 cc (152.4 cu in) N52B25 I6 producing 150 kW (204 PS; 201 hp) and 245 N·m (181 lb·ft). The sDrive30i is powered by the 2,996 cc (182.8 cu in) N52B30 I6 producing 190 kW (258 PS; 255 hp) and 300 N·m (221 lb·ft). The sDrive35i is powered by a 2,979 cc (181.8 cu in) N54B30 twin-turbocharged I6 producing 225 kW (306 PS; 302 hp) and 400 N·m (295 lb·ft). The new roadster features a completely revamped interior, designed by Nadya Arnaout, and exterior, designed by Juliana Blasi, a retractable hardtop, and an optional 7-speed double clutch transmission. It is also the first BMW roadster to use iDrive. Compared to the previous generation Z4, the new vehicle has grown 148 mm (5.8 in) longer, 9 mm (0.4 in) wider, 2.5 mm (0.098 in) in wheelbase, and is significantly heavier, adding between 150 kg (330 lb) and 235 kg (520 lb) in unladen weight, when compared to the previous model.The 204 hp 2.5-liter Z4 can reach 0-62 mph in 6.6 seconds, and hit a top speed of 151 mph, while to more powerful 3.0-liter engine gets 258 hp, which allows it to run from 0-62 mph in 5.8 seconds and keep going up to an electronically limited top speed of 155 mph. The top-of-the-line sDrive35i model will sprint the 0-62 mph run in 5.1 seconds.

BUGATTI VEYRON

The Bugatti Veyron EB 16.4 is a mid-engine grand touring car produced by Bugatti headquarters in Château St Jean in Molsheim (Alsace, France), and whose production and development is often credited to Ferdinand Karl Piech. It is named after French racing driver Pierre Veyron, who won the 24 hours of Le Mans in 1939 while racing for the original Bugatti company. Two hundred examples of the Veyron are known to have been built and delivered since production began. There will be a total of 300 built. The editions that are contributing are the Veyron, Veyron 16.4, Pur Sang, Hermes Edition, Sang Noir, Targa, Vincero, and the Bleu Centenaire. It will be replaced with the Grand Sport, which is essentially a Veyron Convertible. According to Volkswagen (and approved by TÜV Süddeutschland), the final production Veyron engine produces 1,001 hp (746 kW) and gives 1,250 N·m (920 ft·lbf) of torque. The horsepower figure has been confirmed by Bugatti officials to actually be conservative, with the real total being 1010 or more. The car's everyday top speed is listed at 350 km/h (220 mph). When the car reaches 220 km/h (140 mph), hydraulics lower the car until it has a ground clearance of about 8.9 cm (3 inches). At the same time, the wing and spoiler deploy. This is the "handling mode", in which the wing helps provide 3,425 newtons (770 lbf) of downforce, holding the car to the road. The Veyron costs Euro 1,100,000 (net price without taxes); prices vary by exchange rates and local taxes (like value added taxes). Prices for the UK or the US are over £880,000, or around $1,400,000.

CADILLAC CTS

GM revealed the all-new 2008 CTS at the North American International Auto Show in January 2007. The base model featured a 3.6 L variable valve timing V6 with 258 hp (192 kW) and 252 lb·ft (342 N·m) of torque. A second engine, a new 3.6 L direct-injection V6 VVT engine with 304 hp (227 kW) and 274 foot-pounds force (371 N·m) of torque was also offered. The new car came with a six-speed manual transmission as standard equipment, with GM's six-speed Hydra-matic 6L50 automatic transmission available as an option on all variants. On-demand all-wheel drive was offered with both engines when equipped with an automatic transmission. Suspension, braking, and steering improvements from the previous generation CTS-V were designed into the new standard CTS.The second generation was wider and longer than the original, measuring 191.6 inches (4866 mm) long, 72.5 inches (1841 mm) wide and 58 inches (1472 mm) in height. Wheelbase remained unchanged at 113.4 inches (2880 mm), but with a wider front/rear track of 61.8 / 62.0 inches (1575 / 1585 mm), donated by the larger STS. Other changes included a tweaked exterior, with a new, larger grille, slimmer headlights and taillights, side air extractor vents located forward of the front doors, and new nine-spoke 18-inch wheels, surrounding larger high-performance brake calipers and rotors. Available features on the second-gen CTS included a Bose 5.1 surround sound system, GM's Stabilitrak ESC system, a tire pressure monitoring system, a navigation system with real-time traffic and weather data, an integrated 40 GB hard drive for music storage, swiveling headlights, and remote starting. In 2008, the CTS was selected as the car that would re-launch the Cadillac brand in Australia and New Zealand.

CHEVROLET CAMARO

Based on the 2006 Camaro Concept and 2007 Camaro Convertible Concept, production of the fifth-generation Camaro was approved on 10 August 2006. Oshawa Car Assembly produces the new Camaro which went on sale in spring of 2009 as a 2010 model year vehicle. The 2010 model is offered as a coupe only in LS, LT, and SS trim levels. The LS and LT trim levels are powered by the LLT 3.6L (217ci) V6 producing 304 hp (227 kW). The SS is powered by the LS3 6.2L (376ci) V8 producing 426 hp (318 kW) when paired with the 6 speed manual. When paired with the 6 speed automatic the L99 V8 producing 400 hp (300 kW) is installed. The 5th generation Camaro was used as Bumblebee in the movie Transformers. The RS appearance package is available on both the LT and SS. Production began on 16 March 2009 as a 2010 model. Motor Trend has called it "The best new car from Chevrolet in over 30 years". Its competitors are the Dodge Challenger and the Ford Mustang GT. Chevy plans a supercharged Z-28 version, although no official specs or timeline has been addressed by GM. The Camaro continues to find its way into modern day fiction. The vehicle mode of the character Bumblebee in the 2007 film, Transformers, is first a 1976 model Camaro and later a fifth-generation concept variant. A modified fifth-generation Camaro reprises the role of Bumblebee in the sequel, Transformers: Revenge of the Fallen.

CHEVROLET CORVETTE ZR1

The C6 ZR1 is a high performance version of the C6 Chevrolet Corvette. It is the fastest and most powerful Corvette ever produced. The ZR1 engine is a modified LS3, designated the LS9, producing 638 hp (476 kW) and 604 ft·lbf (819 N·m). of torque. The LS9 has a sixth-generation Eaton TVS R2300 roots 4-lobe supercharger with an intercooler. The ZR1 flywheel has been improved over the 2008 Zo6. The flywheel was upgraded by going from six to a nine bolt design and cutting off nearly 9.8 ounces for improved throttle response and acceleration. The transmission is a 6-speed manual Tremec TR6060 with a MH3 gearset. The 2008 Zo6 featured the MM6 gearset. The name of the ride control system is Magnetic Selective Ride Control (MSRC). MSRC is provided by Delphi. The system uses two modes of control: Tour and Sport.The system offers standing start launch modifications. When launching the ZR1 from a standing start, the shocks are completely softened on launch and stiffened on rebound. The softened shocks on launch aid the ZR1 by allowing weight to transfer to the rear, aiding traction. The ride control standing launch modifications are designed to minimize bounce. The chassis, similar to the 2008 Zo6, is made of aluminum. To cut weight, many panels are made of carbon fiber. Panels made of carbon fiber are the fenders, hood, roof, splitter, and rocker extensions. To prevent the sun from damaging the carbon fiber, panels are protected with a special paint treatment. The rear wheels are the largest ever mounted on a production Corvette with 335/25 Michelin Pilot Sport PS2 tires on ultra-light 20 in (510 mm) rims.The official curb weight of the 2009 ZR1 was released to be 3,352 lb (1,520 kg).

CHEVROLET VOLT

The Chevrolet Volt is a plug-in hybrid electric vehicle to be produced by General Motors, expected to be launched as a 2011 model. Sales are scheduled to begin in November 2010, and in spite of GM bankruptcy filing, the automaker announced it remained committed to keeping the Volt on schedule. The Volt's propulsion system will be based on GM's new Voltec (formerly known as E-Flex) platform, which differs significantly from GM's earlier BAS Hybrid and Two-Mode Hybrid systems. The electric power for the vehicle is sourced from its onboard lithium-ion batteries which are charged by an electrical power outlet and/or the gasoline engine. The Volt's 16 kWh lithium-ion battery pack can be fully charged (technically ~85%; see SOC) by plugging the car into a 120-240VAC residential electrical outlet using the provided SAE J1772 compliant charging cord. No external charging station will be required. Unlike most current commercially available electric hybrids, the actual propulsion of the Volt is accomplished exclusively by the electric motor, and the internal combustion engine is used as another charging method. With fully charged batteries, enough stored electrical energy will power the Volt for 40 miles (64 km), a distance capable of satisfying the daily commute of 75% of Americans, which averages around 33 miles (53 km). After 40 miles (64 km), a small 4-cylinder gasoline internal combustion engine drives a 53 kW generator effectively extending the Volt's potential range to as much as 640 miles (1,030 km) on a single tank of gasoline. The electrical power from the generator is sent to either the electric motor or the batteries, depending on the state of charge (SOC) of the battery pack and the power demanded at the wheels. The distribution is controlled by the electronic control unit (ECU) of the vehicle.

DODGE CHALLENGER SRT-8

On December 3, 2007, Chrysler started taking deposits for the third-generation Dodge Challenger which debuted on February 6, 2008 simultaneously at the Chicago Auto Show and Philadelphia International Auto Show. Listing at US$40,095, the new version is a 2-door coupe which shares common design elements with the first generation Challenger, despite being significantly longer and taller. The chassis is a modified (shortened wheelbase) version of the LX platform that underpins the 2006-Current Dodge Charger, 2005-2008 Dodge Magnum, and the 2005-Current Chrysler 300. All 2008 models were SRT8s and equipped with the 6.1 L (370 cu in) Hemi and a 5-speed AutoStick automatic transmission, which outperforms the legendary 1970 Hemi Challenger. The entire 2008 run of 6,400 cars were pre-sold (many of which for above MSRP), and production commenced on May 8, 2008. Chrysler Canada is offering the Canada 500 and Chrysler of Mexico is offering only 100 of this car for that country with a 6.1 liter engine and 425 brake horsepower (317 kW) (SAE); the version is SRT/8. Chrysler auctioned off two 2008 SRT8 for charity with car #1 going for $400,000.00 to benefit the notMYkid non-profit organization, and a "B5" Blue #43 car fetching a winning bid of $228,143.43 with the proceeds going to Victory Junction Gang Camp. The 2009 SRT8, while still equipped with the 6.1L Hemi V8, is virtually identical to its 2008 counterpart, with the main difference being the choice of either a 5-speed automatic or a 6-speed manual transmission. Standard features include Brembo brakes, a sport suspension, bi-xenon headlamps, heated leather sport seats, keyless go, Sirius satellite radio, and 20-inch (510 mm) forged aluminum wheels. In addition, the 2009 will have a true "limited slip" differential.

FERRARI 599 GTB FIORANO

The 599 GTB Fiorano (internal code F139) is an Italian gran turismo. It is Ferrari's two-seat flagship, replacing the 575 M Maranello in 2006 as a 2007 model. Styled by Pininfarina under the direction of Ferrari's Frank Stephenson, the 599 GTB debuted at the Geneva Motor Show in February 2006. It is named for its total engine displacement (5999 cc), Gran Turismo Berlinetta nature, and the Fiorano Circuit test track used by Ferrari. The Tipo F133F 6.0 L (5999 cc) V12 engine produces a maximum 620 PS (456 kW; 612 hp), making it the most powerful series production Ferrari road car. Its 608 N·m (448 ft·lbf) of torque will also be a high for Ferrari's GT cars. Most of the modifications to the engine were done to allow it to fit in the Fiorano's engine bay (the original Enzo version could be taller as it would not block forward vision due to its mid-mounted position). The company claims a top speed in excess of 330 km/h (205 mph), 0–100 km/h (62 mph) in 3.7 seconds, and 11.0 seconds to 200 km/h (124 mph). The 599XX version, is a car designed for track use, based on the 599 GTB. The 599XX engine's maximum speed has been increased to 9000rpm with the engine rated 700 PS (690 hp/515 kW)@9000rpm. The weight has been reduced by cutting the weight of the engine unit components, and extensive use of composites and carbon-fibre body parts, and carbon-fibre brake pads. for this model a new gearbox shift strategy has been implemented, introduced to cut overall gear change time to 60 ms. Aerodynamics on the 599XX were retuned to give more downforce (280 kg @ 200 km/h, 630 kg @ 300 km/h). The car also includes 29/67 R19 front and 31/71 R19 rear tires with 19 x 11J wheel rims at the front and 19 x 12J at the rear.

FERRARI CALIFORNIA

The Ferrari California is a grand touring sports car that was launched by Ferrari at the 2008 Paris Motor Show. It is a two door "2+2" hard top convertible. The California is powered by front-mid mounted gasoline direct injection 4.3 L (260 cu in) V8, sending a claimed 338 kW (460 PS; 453 hp) to the rear wheels. The car revives the "California" name used for the late-1950s Ferrari 250 GT.

The California will be built in a new production line adjacent to the existing factory at Maranello. The existing production line produces 27 cars per day, or 6,000 per annum. Ferrari plans to produce 5,000 Californias in the first two years of production, thereby increasing Ferrari production by 50% with introduction of the model.. The model, according to many motoring magazines, is sold out until 2012

The California has a top speed of 310 km/h (193 mph) and it can accelerate from zero to 100 km/h (62 mph) under 4 seconds. Although 285 kilograms (628 lb) heavier and 30 PS (30 hp/22 kW) less powerful than the mid-engined Ferrari F430, the California reaches 60 mph (97 km/h) in the same time as the F430 thanks to the dual-clutch transmission.

Ferrari spent over 1,000 hours in the wind tunnel with a one-third-scale model of the California perfecting its aerodynamics. With the top up, the California has a drag coefficient of 0.32, making it the most aerodynamic Ferrari ever made.

FORD HARLEY-DAVIDSON F150

The F-Series was the best-selling vehicle in the United States for 23 years and has been the best-selling truck for 31 years. In the 10th generation of the F-series, Ford split the F-150 & F-250/350 into two different body styles. The new F-250/F-350 and as of 2007 F-450 is called the Super Duty. Ford revealed the next generation 2009 F-150 design at the North American International Auto Show in January, 2008. The truck features a larger and more flexible interior, an updated three-bar grille, and additional choices of cab styles and trim levels. The chassis includes a lighter-weight, high strength steel for better fuel economy and safety and improved payload and towing capacity. Three engines are initially offered with the 2009 redesign: a revised 5.4 L 3-valve Triton V8 that is E85 capable with a new output rating of 320 hp (239 kW) and 395 lb·ft (529 N·m) of torque, a 292 hp (218 kW) 4.6 L 3-valve V8, and a 248 hp (185 kW) 4.6 L 2-valve V8. The 3-valve 5.4 and 4.6 liter V8s are mated to Ford's new 6R80E 6-speed automatic transmission while the 4R75E 4-speed automatic transmission used previously is carried over for the 2-valve 4.6 L V8. Additional engine offerings under development and projected for the 2010 model year include a new 4.4 L diesel V8 with a projected 330 hp (246 kW) and 400 lb·ft (569N·m) of torque and an Ecoboost gas turbocharged direct injection 3.5 L DOHC V6. On February 10, 2009 at the Chicago Auto Show, the latest and 14th since 2000 edition of the F-150 was introduced. Adopting many luxury features of the Platinum Edition, the Harley Davidson special edition went one step further by providing leather seating surfaces derived from authentic Harley biker-jacket materials, as well as the requisite exhaust tones and power to reach a top speed of 115 mph (185 km/h).

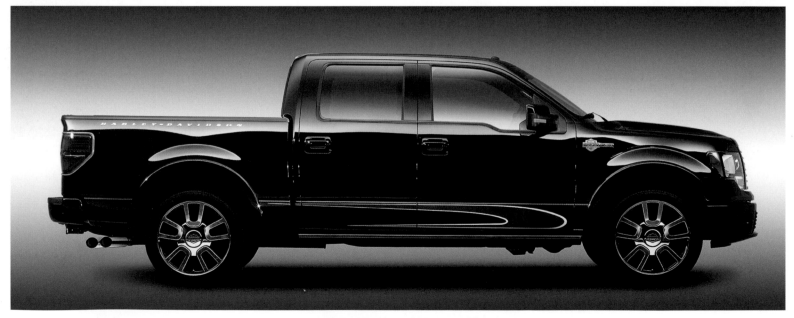

FORD SHELBY GT500

The Shelby Mustang is a high performance variant of the Ford Mustang, built from 1968 through 1970. The 1965, 1966 and 1967 From 1968 the model became the Shelby Cobra GT. The program was factory-sponsored by Ford to compete with the Corvette, also factory-sponsored by Chevrolet, neither of which could be built for the sales price charged. In 2007, following the introduction of the Fifth-generation Ford Mustang the Shelby nameplate was revived for new high performance versions of the Mustang. The Ford Shelby GT500KR, revealed at the 2007 New York International Auto Show, was released in the spring of 2008. The car is powered by a 540 horsepower 5.4-liter (330 CID) supercharged V-8 Racing Power Upgrade Pack. SVT and Shelby announced that 1,000 40th Anniversary Editions will be built for the U.S. in 2008, with another 571 units in 2009. This 1,571 production run matches that of the original 1968 GT500KR. In total, 1,746 units will be produced, with the extra 175 units going to other markets. The Shelby GT500KR features a carbon composite hood with scoops and hood pins, a lowered front air dam, and 14-inch (360 mm) Brembo brand front brakes with functional cooling ducts. The suspension has been modified and tuned by Shelby Automobiles and Ford Racing including unique spring rates, dampers, stabilizer bars, and strut tower brace, all designed specifically for the KR. The GT500KR draws on styling features from the classic 1968 "King of the Road" GT500KR model.The GT500KR's price will be $79,995. The GT500KR is featured prominently in the new Knight Rider television series on NBC. One of the main characters of the show is KITT, an advanced Artificial Intelligence housed in a GT500KR. Also, in the return of the show, KARR is also a GT500KR.

HYUNDAI GENESIS COUPE

The Hyundai Genesis Coupe is a rear-wheel drive sports coupe from Hyundai Motor Company, released on October 13, 2008 for the Korean market. It is Hyundai's first rear-wheel drive sports coupe, and shares its basic platform with the Hyundai Genesis luxury sedan. The Genesis Coupe arrived in United States dealerships on February 26, 2009 as a 2010 model. Hyundai USA acting President and CEO John Krafcik has described the Genesis Coupe as being designed "...to deliver a driving experience that challenges cars like Infiniti G37." Hyundai has stated the Genesis Coupe is not a successor to the Hyundai Tiburon. According to Korean newspaper Autotimes, Hyundai is also ready to release the new Tiburon, which has a 1.6 L/2.0 L Turbo Engine.Hyundai released the full specs for the Genesis Coupe on October 30, 2008. There are 9 models of the Coupe ranging from 5 Turbos and 4 V6's. There is the 2.0T Base, 2.0T Premium, 2.0T Grand Touring, 2.0T Track (GT in Canada), 2.0T R-Spec, 3.8 Base, 3.8 Premium, 3.8 Grand Touring, and a 3.8 Track (GT in Canada) editions. The track and R-Spec versions in the 2.0T will only be 6 speed manual. The R-spec 2.0T comes with stability control, ABS, electronic brake force distribution, 19-inch wheels, Brembo brakes, a Torsen limited-slip differential, a beefier suspension and summer-only Potenzas. To reduce cost and weight, the R-Spec doesn't include Bluetooth, automatic headlights, cruise control, trip computer, chrome interior accents and steering wheel audio controls. The Genesis Coupe R-Spec will be available mid-2010 with a base price $3,000 less than the 2.0T Track model. The gas mileage is for the 2.0T is EPA 30 mpg-US (7.8 L/100 km; 36 mpg-imp) highway, and a EPA rating of 25 mpg-US (9.4 L/100 km; 30 mpg-imp) for the 3.8.

JAGUAR XFR

The production version of the XF debuted at the 2007 Frankfurt Motor Show. In January 2008, the XF was awarded the prestigious What Car? Car of the Year award, as well as taking away the prize in the executive car category. The XF's entire body was developed using Computational Fluid Dynamics (CFD) before the car ever saw a wind tunnel. Every area from the outer skin to the lightweight, composite undertray to the cooling airflow (even the shape of the exterior mirrors) was optimised using this process. The higher, squarer tail is more efficient aerodynamically than a lower, rounded one, and the XF's coupe-like roofline and raised bootlid lip improve airflow over the rear of the car. As a result, the XF has the best aerodynamic performance, in terms of drag, of any production Jaguar ever and is better than the race-bred, limited edition XJ220 supercar. The XF's drag coefficient is just 0.29, and the front-to-rear lift balance is precisely zero. This aerodynamic performance minimizes wind noise, reduces fuel consumption, and aids strong high-speed stability and handling. The Jaguar XFR, has a new AJ-V8 GenIII engine, which is supercharged and has been bored out to 5.0 litres (from 4.2 litres from the standard version). The car has a acceleration of 0-60 mph in 4.7 seconds, and hit a top speed near to 200 mph (320 km/h). The car has new bumpers, air intakes, sills, grills, tailpipes, a boot-lid spoiler, and has special 20-inch (510 mm) alloy wheels. A "tweaked" XFR, producing 600 bhp (450 kW), hit a top speed of 225.675 mph (363.189 km/h) on Bonneville Salt Flats in November 2008.

JAGUAR XKR

Currently in its second generation, the XK8 was the first 8 cylinder vehicle produced by Jaguar, when the Jaguar AJ-V8 engine was introduced. It used the new all-aluminium monocoque chassis developed from the 2005 Advanced Lightweight Coupé (ALC) concept car and is offered as both a coupé or convertible. In the opposite manner to the way convertibles are traditionally designed, the coupé is based on the convertible. This meant that the engineers could design the convertible without the drawbacks of the car looking like, and actually being, a coupé with the top chopped off. It also meant that minimal additional weight was required to maintain the structural rigidity lost with the removal of the roof (1,635 kg (3,600 lb) kerb weight for the convertible versus 1,595 kg (3,520 lb) for the coupé). This makes the XK convertible exceptionally rigid and lightweight for a car of its type, offering an extremely impressive driving experience. It features a conventional cloth top that will open or close in 18 seconds. The XKR Portfolio was released in early 2007 featuring exclusive Celestial Black paint and 20-inch (510 mm) Cremona five-spoke alloy wheels. In 2009 an all new 5.0 Litre V8 version is available. Interior enhancements included, as standard, an engine-spun aluminium veneer, or an optional Satin American Walnut veneer. The XKR Portfolio also benefits from an upgraded sound system from Bowers & Wilkins, featuring high-output, low-distortion Kevlar mid-range speakers and specially designed aluminium-dome tweeters.There were no performance enhancements to the 4.2 litre supercharged engine, however the brakes were substantially upgraded with the use of Alcon 6-piston callipers on 400 mm (16 in) crescent-grooved discs at the front, and 4-piston callipers on 350 mm (14 in) discs at the rear.

KOENIGSEGG CCX

Koenigsegg began the CCX project with the aim of entering the world market, though particularly the United States car market. Development engineer Magnus Jaasund said "We wanted to go into the world market, but we couldn't do it with the old car." To sell cars to the North American market many alterations were made to the design of the CCR; the previously used Ford Modular engine was replaced by a Koenigsegg engine designed to run on 91 octane fuel, readily available in the United States, and to meet the Californian emission standards. The front bumper of the CCX is designed to be safer in low speed collisions than previous Koenigseggs and the whole body is 3.46 in (88 millimeters) longer to comply with the United States' rear impact regulations. Additionally the CCX can display United States or European number plates. The CCX is 1.6 in (40.6 mm) taller than the CCR and, combined with the carbon fiber reinforced plastic sports seats by Sparco, the CCX allows for 2 in (50.8 mm) of extra headroom that Autoweek reviewer Mark Vaughn hypothesizes is "to accommodate U.S. NBA stars." The electronic control unit has also received an upgrade over the CCR meaning that the CCX is without physical fuses and it is lighter than the previous system. The CCX can accelerate from 0–62 mph (100 km/h) in 3.2 seconds and from 0–124 mph (200 km/h) in 9.8 seconds. According to Koenigsegg it has a top speed of 259 mph (417 km/h), although this has not been officially verified. On 15 June 2008, a standard fully equipped CCX was independently timed by sport auto in achieving a record 0-186-0 mph (0-300-0 km/h) in 29.2 seconds, beating SLR McLaren 722, Lamborghini Murcielago LP640, Porsche 997 GT2, Alpina B6 S, Corvette Z06.

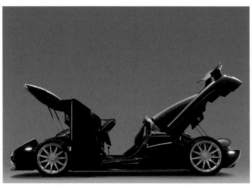

LAMBORGHINI LP560-4

The Lamborghini Gallardo is a sports car built by Lamborghini. The Gallardo is Lamborghini's most-produced model to date, with over 5000 on first three years of production . Each car costs about $180,000 to $210,000. The car is named after a famous breed of fighting bull. The Spanish word gallardo translates into "gallant," and from Italian into "striking". It is powered by a new 5.2L V10 with gasoline direct injection, with improved power and torque. The engine is heavily based on the new Audi RS6 V10. Unlike the precedent engine, this engine no longer has split crankpins, so it is not even firing, but Lamborghini says that due to the stiffer crankshaft it has less vibrations than the previous engine.Transmission choices include six-speed manual or a six-speed E-gear, with E-gear revised to change gears by a rotational selector instead of a fore/aft movement, which offers 40% quicker shifts. E-gear also added Corsa setting and Thrust Mode launch control system.The car was also 20 kg (44 lb) lighter than 2008 base Gallardo. Other changes include a new front bumper influenced by the Murcielago and Lamborghini Reventón.Gallardo LP560-4 has base price of US$198,000, but can go over $322,000 with e-gear, carbon ceramic brakes, navigation and other options. Other factory options are available with Ad Personam program. British version has MSRP of £147,330.00 ($288,943 USD), including NavTrak vehicle tracking system and delivery package.The vehicle was unveiled at 2008 Geneva Auto Show.

LEXUS IS

The Lexus IS is a series of entry-level luxury cars/compact executive cars sold since 1999. Originally sold under the Toyota Altezza (the word "altezza" is Italian for "noble") nameplate in Japan until the introduction of the second generation Lexus IS design. The Altezza name is still used at times to refer to chromed car tail lights like those fitted to the first generation model, known as 'Altezza lights' or 'Lexus-style' lights. The first generation Altezza (codename XE10) was launched in Japan in October 1998, while the Lexus IS 200 (JCE10) made its debut in Europe in 1999 and in North America as the IS 300 in 2000. The first generation, inline-6-powered IS featured sedan and wagon variants. The second generation IS (GSE20) was launched globally in 2006 with V6-powered IS 250 and IS 350 sedan models. A high-performance V8 sedan version, the IS F, premiered in 2007. Hardtop convertible versions, the IS 250 C and IS 350 C, debuted in 2008. According to Lexus, the IS designation stands for Intelligent Sport. The IS was completely redesigned for the 2006 model year and began arriving at dealerships in the fall of 2005. A pre-production car of the second generation IS model was shown at the 2005 Geneva Auto Show, with the production version debuting at the 2006 New York Auto Show. The new IS was the second debut of Lexus' new L-finesse design philosophy on a production vehicle, following the premiere of the 2006 Lexus GS performance sedan which it also shares a platform with. The new IS design featured sleeker, coupe-like contours, a fastback profile, and a repeated arrowhead motif in the front fascia and side windows. The forward design was reminiscent of the earlier Lexus LF-C coupe concept. The new IS body resulted in a 0.28 Cd figure.

LOTUS EVORA

The Evora is the first product of a five year plan started in 2006 to expand the Lotus line of cars. As such it is a larger car than recent Lotus models Elise and its derivatives (Exige, Europa S, etc.), weighing an estimated kerb weight of 1350 kg (2976 lb). It is currently the only Lotus model with a 2+2 configuration, although it has been announced that it will also be offered in a two-seater configuration, referred to as the "Plus Zero" option. It is also the only 2+2 mid engined coupé on sale. Powered by a Lotus-tuned 3.5-liter V6 engine producing 276 hp, and weighing just 2,976 lbs. While for Lotus top speed is of less importance than stability at speed, early indications suggest a maximum speed of 160 mph and the ability to sprint from 0-60 mph in under 5 seconds The Evora offers a more refined ownership experience than Lotus's existing smaller four-cylinder models with a contemporary, hand-crafted and elegantly trimmed cabin and an equipment list including such high-tech features as an advanced touch-screen multi-media system incorporating a state-of-the-art Alpine satellite navigation and audio system. The interior is larger to allow taller persons to fit, such as Lotus CEO Mike Kimberley, and two 99th percentile (6'5") American males. The cooled boot behind the engine is large enough to fit a set of golf clubs, although Lotus Design Head Russell Carr denies that this was intentional. Lotus intends the Evora to compete with different market sectors including the Porsche Cayman. The name "Evora" keeps the Lotus tradition of beginning model names with an "E". The name was a random derivative of the term Evo,Sales are expected to start in summer 2009. The sales target is 2000 cars per year, with prices between £45,000 and just over £50,000.

LOTUS EXIGE S

The Lotus Exige is a two-door, two-seat sports car made by Lotus Cars. It is essentially a coupe version of the Lotus Elise, which is a roadster that is mid-engined and has been in production since 1996.

The original Exige (NA or naturally aspirated Exige) was launched in 2000 and had a 1.8 L Rover K Series engine in VHPD (Very High Performance Derivative) tune. It produced 177 bhp (132 kW; 179 PS) in standard form and 192 bhp (143 kW; 195 PS) in the "track spec" version.

In 2004, the Series 2 Exige was introduced. It features a 1.8 L 16-valve DOHC Toyota/Yamaha engine that produces 190 bhp (142 kW; 193 PS) with the Toyota engine designation of 2ZZ-GE. Compared to the Series 2 Elise, it has a front splitter, fibreglass hardtop roof with roof scoop, rear engine cover, and rear spoiler. The sole purpose of these aerodynamic additions to the base Elise is to create more downforce (almost 100 lb (45 kg) of downforce at 100 mph (160 km/h) in the Exige versus 13 lb (5.9 kg) at 100 mph (160 km/h) in the Elise).

In 2009 model year, Exige will be offered in the United States in two configurations: S240 and S260. S240 is the continuation of the 2008 model, it weighs 2,077 lb (942 kg) and comes with a 240 hp (180 kW) supercharged engine. New for 2009, S260 weighs 2,020 lb (920 kg) with a full tank of fuel; its engine has been improved to produce 257 hp (192 kW) and 0–60 mph (0–97 km/h) acceleration in 4.0 seconds. Base manufacturer suggested retail prices for S240 and S260 are $65,690 and $74,995, respectively.

MASERATI GRANTURISMO S

The Maserati GranTurismo is a grand tourer produced by Italian automaker Maserati. Officially presented at the Geneva Motor Show in March 2007, the two-door 2+2 coupé is powered by a wet sump Ferrari/Maserati V8. The GranTurismo S is powered by a 4.7 liter V8 in place of the regular GT's 4.2 liter unit. Output is 433 horsepower at 7,000 rpm with a torque number of 360 lb-ft at 4,750 rpm, improvements of 28 and 21, respectively. In the S, an advanced MC-Shift dual-clutch transmission replaces the ZF six-speed automatic. The changes result in a top speed for the S of 183 mph, up from 177 mph and the 62 mph arrives from a standstill nearly three-tenths of a second quicker, at 4.93. Due to the transaxle configuration, the weight distribution of the S is more rear-biased, at 53 percent, compared to the regular car's 51 percent rear bias. New high-power Brembo brakes improve stopping distance and offer higher resistance to fade. Maserati claims the car can stop from 62 mph in less than 115 feet. The system features front brake discs made with dual-cast technology, resulting in pairing up iron and aluminum for better weight, heat transfer properties, and squeezed by aluminum mono-bloc 6-piston calipers. The S rides on unique 20-inch wheels, as opposed to the GT's 19s.

Other exterior visual distinctions between the two are unique side skirts and an integrated spoiler. The dimensions of the GranTurismo and S are virtually identical, though the S is 2.7 inches wider.

MAYBACH ZEPPELIN

The **legendary Maybach Zeppelin, which** was revered worldwide as the ultimate in high-class automotive engineering in the 1930s. The new model's performance even outclasses the rest of the Maybach range, making it the most powerful Maybach ever. The Maybach 57 S and the long-wheelbase version, the 62 S, serve as the technical basis for the new range-topping model. Supreme performance by the 6.0 litre V12 biturbo power unit under the bonnet, which now delivers 471 kW/640 hp (+ 28 hp) and a peak torque of 1000 Newton metres. From the outside, the luxury brand's new top-of-the-range model can be recognised by its two-tone special paint finish. The shoulderline is painted right through to the background of the headlamp assemblies in Rocky Mountains light brown, which forms a stylish and scintillating contrast to the Taiga black finish used for the rest of the vehicle body. Dark red tail light units and a fine vertical partition in the tailpipe add striking visual touches at the rear. The Maybach Zeppelin's newly designed 20-inch wheels in a Chrome Shadow finish complete the picture. The streamlined exterior mirrors, which produce even less wind noise, are new to Maybach. They have a more angular design and are separated from the door frame by a slender arm.Finest-quality leather and high-gloss piano lacquer trim The new Maybach Zeppelin is a car for connoisseurs, as is immediately apparent from its interior. Here, the luxurious leather appointments in California beige leather form a delightful contrast with the exclusive leather in deep Stromboli black.World first – a system for a fine interior fragrance Customers are also able to opt for an especially refined equipment detail that is exclusive to the Maybach Zeppelin – an imaginatively designed, extremely high-quality perfume atomiser, the only one of its kind in the world.

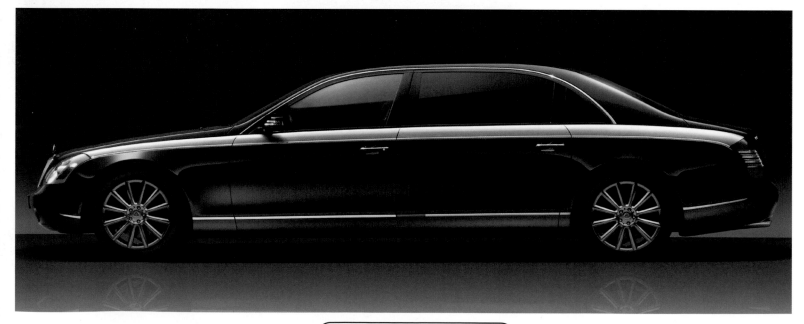

MERCEDES S CLASS

The S-Class, a product of nine lines of Mercedes-Benz models dating since the mid-1950s, is the world's best-selling luxury flagship sedan. As the foremost model in the Mercedes-Benz lineup, the S-Class has debuted many of the company's latest innovations, including drivetrain technologies, interior features, and safety systems. The latest generation, the W221 S-Class, premiered in 2006 as an all-new design. As in previous iterations, the latest S-Class is sold in standard and long wheelbase versions and offers V6, V8, V12, and diesel powertrains. The name "S-Class" derives from the German word "Sonderklasse" of which "S-Class" is an abbreviation. Sonderklasse means "special class" and in automotive terms thus refers to "a specially outfitted car." Past two-door coupe models of the S-Class were known as SEC and later S Coupe. In 1998 they were spun off in a separate line as the CL-Class, however it will be re-designated as the S-Coupe when launching the mid-generational facelift/refresh of the C216 later in 2009 as a 2010 model. The latest S-Class is slightly larger in all dimensions than its predecessor, and it features three newly developed engines with up to 26% power increase. The interior is completely new, all materials have been upgraded and make for a more luxurious ride, and the center console transmission gear lever has been replaced with a column-mounted shifter. Models sold in North America are the S450 (2008-,SWB and Canada only), S550, S600, S63 AMG and S65 AMG; other models to be sold outside North America include the S280, S350, S300, S420 CDI and S320 CDI. The first W221 model released in North America and Japan was the S550 (called S500 outside North America and Japan), with the S600 arriving in the following spring.

MERCEDES-BENZ SL65 AMG BLACK

The Mercedes-Benz SL is a roadster manufactured by Mercedes since 1954.

The designation SL derives from the German Sport Leicht, or Sport Light — and was first applied to the 300SL 'Gullwing' named also after its "gullwing" or upward-opening doors. It is also one of the world's safest sport vehicles.

The term SL-Class refers to the marketing variations of the vehicle, including the numerous engine configurations spanning five design generations.

The new SL65 AMG Black Series coupe features a carbon-fiber fixed roof, front fenders, hood, trunk lid, and front and rear aprons. With the absence of retractable roof hardware, the car is more than 550 pounds lighter than the standard SL. AMG placed a modified version of the 6.0-liter AMG V12 engine that now delivers 670 bhp (500 kW) and 738 lb·ft (1,001 N·m) of torque. This engine has been labeled as the engine with the largest output that will be made by AMG.

Its twin turbochargers are 12 percent larger, passages for intake air and the turbo wastegates have been modified, and the intake air intercooler is 30 percent more efficient. The result is 0-to-60 mph (97 km/h) acceleration of 3.8 seconds, and an electronically limited top speed of 198 mph (319 km/h).

MERCEDES MCLAREN SLR 722 EDITION

The Mercedes-Benz SLR McLaren is an Anglo-German supercar jointly developed by Mercedes-Benz and McLaren Automotive, built in Portsmouth and the McLaren Technology Centre in Woking, Surrey, England. SLR stands for "Sport, Leicht, Rennsport" (sport, light, racing). Mercedes-Benz has stated that they will build 3500 SLRs in a span of 7 years, with an annual production of 500 cars. The car's base price is GB£300,000 (approx. US$495,000). However demand was insufficient to meet targeted sales numbers, production will end in 2009 as planned A new version was introduced in 2006 called the Mercedes-Benz SLR McLaren 722 Edition. The "722" refers to the victory by Stirling Moss and his co-driver Denis Jenkinson in a Mercedes-Benz 300 SLR with the starting number 722 (indicating a start time of 7:22 a.m.) at the Mille Miglia in 1955. The "722 Edition" boosts power to 650 PS (478 kW; 641 hp) and 820 N·m (605 lb·ft) of torque at 4000 rpm, posting a top speed of 337 km/h (209 mph) (just 3 km/h faster than the standard SLR). 19-inch light-alloy wheels were used to reduce unsprung weight, while modifications were also made to the suspension, with a stiffer damper setup and 10 mm (0.4 in) lower ride height introduced for improved handling. Larger 390 mm (15.4 in) diameter front brakes and a revised front air dam and rear diffuser were fitted. Exterior changes, other than the larger 19-inch (480 mm) black light-alloy wheels, include red "722" badging, hearkening back to the original 722 racer, and slightly different taillights and headlamps. The SLR 722 can go from 0 to 100 km/h (62 mph) km/h in 3.6 seconds, 200 km/h (124 mph) in 10.2 seconds and 300 km/h (186 mph) in 21.4 seconds and can reach a top speed of 337 km/h (209 mph).

NISSAN GT-R SPEC V

Nissan introduced the GT-R SpecV on January 7, 2009 at the 2009 Tokyo Auto Salon. Exterior changes from the base GT-R consist of a carbon fiber rear spoiler, grille, and brake ducts, along with an exclusive Ultimate Black Opal paint job. Interior changes include a set of carbon fiber Recaro front seats with the rear seats being completely removed. Carbon fiber covers the center storage box, instrument panel, and replaces the majority of the interior trim.

The GT-R SpecV is powered by the standard twin-turbo 3,799 cc (3.8 L; 231.8 cu in) V6 with no increase in (peak) horsepower, but a new high gear boost controller that temporarily increases boost pressure should deliver more torque in mid to high-range revs. Other mechanical changes include a titanium exhaust, reworked suspension, carbon ceramic brakes, and 20-inch (510 mm) NISMO wheels. Overall weight is decreased by 132 lb (60 kg) over the standard GT-R.

Japan sales begin on February 2, 2009 at seven pre-selected dealers who are staffed by mechanics with special GT-R SpecV training and are knowledgeable of racing circuit driving. Pricing is set at ¥15,750,000 (over US$160,000). Nissan has not announced any plans to sell the SpecV outside of Japan.

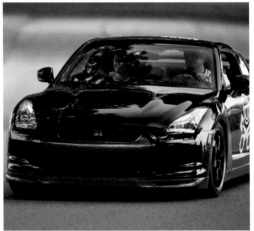

PORSCHE 911 GT3

The Porsche 911 GT3 was introduced in 1999 as a high performance version of the first water-cooled version of the Porsche 911, the 996, to continue the quarter-century tradition of low-weight RS (short for "Rennsport" in German) models that ended with the 993 RS. The GT3, named after the FIA GT class it was intended for, did not use the rather simple engine of the regular production versions of the 996, but a naturally-aspirated version of the turbocharged Porsche 962 and Porsche 911 GT1 race cars. Later, the turbo-charged Porsche 911 GT2 was added to the maker's lineup, but unlike its predecessor 993 GT2, did not fit into GT racing regulations. The racing versions of the GT3 have won several major 24h races outright, and mainly dominated their class at Le Mans. The 911 GT3 competes with the BMW M3 GTR and the Ferrari F430 GT2.

Premiered at this year's Geneva auto show, the 2010 Porsche 911 GT3 is priced just under 100,000 Euros. Powered by a 3.8 liter engine with 435 bhp, the 2010 Porsche 911 GT3 is able to accelerate from 0 to 100 km/h in 4.1 seconds and if you keep your foot on the gas you'll reach a maximum speed of 312 km/h. The 2010 Porsche 911 GT3 features the latest technology of the German sports car manufacturer including the new active PASM suspension and the new Stability Management system

PORSCHE PANAMERA

The Porsche Panamera is a four-door, four-seat luxury sedan, set to be launched in 2009. It will be front-engined and rear wheel drive, with four-wheel drive available on top versions. At launch, the Panamera will have three engine choices - a 3.6 L V6 found in the 2008 facelifted Cayenne with 300 hp (224 kW; 304 PS) in the base Panamera, a 4.8 L V8 with 405 hp (302 kW; 411 PS) in the Panamera S and Panamera 4S, and a turbocharged 4.8 L V8 with approximately 500 hp (373 kW; 507 PS) in the Panamera Turbo. There is even a hybrid version in the pipeline. Rumors suggest that the V-10 engine from Porsche's limited-run Carrera GT supercar may be offered as well, although this is still extremely unlikely given the expense of manufacturing the engine and that Porsche does not currently have a facility capable of producing a suitable number of the V-10 engines per year. It is also rumored that the V-12 diesel from the Audi Q7 may be used in the Panamera. US models include engine start/stop system. Turbo version includes active aerodynamics with a multi-stage, adjustable rear spoiler. The Panamera is being marketed as a sedan, however this is technically inaccurate. It is in fact a five-door hatchback, complete with a wide-opening rear liftgate and more trunk room than a typical sedan. Porsche Traction Management includes fully-controlled all-wheel drive. PTM is standard on both the Panamera 4S and the Panamera Turbo. Optional Sports Chrono Packages includes a Sport Plus button, which includes tighter damping and air springs and drops the car body by 25 mm (0.98 in). The Panamera's name is derived, like the Porsche Carrera line, from the Carrera Panamericana race. Earlier prototypes of four-door sedans such as the 1991 Porsche 989 prototype or the even earlier 4-door 911 based prototype, never went into production.

ROLLS ROYCE PHANTOM COUPE

You've heard the old maxim about not being able to afford something if you have to ask its price, but the fact is some people do ask that question about Rolls-Royce cars, including the new Phantom coupe. The difference between those people and mere mortals who pale at the notion of a $405,000 automobile is that they're asking because they're ready to write a check. That scenario is more likely in the U.S., according to Rolls marketing types. Although part of the Rolls allure is being able to personalize the car in excruciating detail—44,000 possible colors, for example—it's not uncommon for U.S. buyers to walk in and pop for whatever happens to be on the showroom floor—no waiting, drive it home. What they'll be driving home in this case is the newest and sportiest Phantom, and 400 large is what Rolls projects as the base price when it's available here in November. Sporty is always a relative term, particularly when it's applied to a coupe that's well over 18 feet long and weighs close to three tons. So the sporty relativity here is to the other Phantoms—the sedans, standard and long, and the drophead coupe. Power, furnished by a 6.7-liter BMW V-12, is ample: 453 horsepower, 531 pound-feet of torque, enough to propel all that mass to 60 mph in well under six seconds, according to Rolls. Beyond that, the coupe drives smaller than its specs suggest, the suspension is a little stiffer than that of the other Phantoms, and the steering is surprisingly quick and tactile, with good on-center response. Still, this is not a car that begs to be flogged through a series of switchbacks, and it doesn't take much to make the giant 21-inch Goodyears howl in anguish.

SALEEN S7

The Saleen S7 is a limited-production, hand-built, high-performance automobile developed jointly by Saleen, Hidden Creek Industries, Phil Frank Design, and Ray Mallock Ltd. with RML taking full credit designing and developing the S7, and produced solely by Saleen in Irvine, California. It is the first car produced by Saleen not based on an existing design. The S7 debuted on August 19, 2000 at the Monterey Historic Races. From 2000 until 2004, the S7 featured a naturally aspirated V8 engine with 550 horsepower (410 kW). In 2005, the S7 was replaced by the S7 Twin Turbo, which featured a more powerful twin-turbo system that boosted engine power to 750 horsepower (760 PS/559 kW) and the top speed to an estimated 250 mph (402 km/h). The S7 can accelerate from 0-60 miles per hour (97 km/h) in an estimated 2.8 seconds, and to 100 miles per hour in an estimated 8.1 seconds. It can complete a standing quarter mile in an estimated 11.75 seconds, reaching 126 miles per hour (203 km/h). The maximum speed of the car is above 200 miles per hour (322 km/h). The Saleen S7-R is a racing version of the standard, naturally-aspirated S7, produced from 2000 to 2007. It was designed to compete in grand tourer-style motorsports series and events such as the American Le Mans Series, FIA GT Championship, and 24 Hours of Le Mans. Ray Mallock Ltd. built the first few S7-Rs in their workshops in Britain, before Saleen assumed S7-R assembly with the French Oreca squad executing final outfitting in 2006. A total of fourteen S7-Rs have been built so far.

SSC ULTIMATE AERO TT

The SSC Ultimate Aero is an American-built mid-engine sports car by Shelby SuperCars. SSC stands for Shelby SuperCars and TT stands for Twin Turbo. Its higher-performance limited production version, the SSC Ultimate Aero TT, is currently the fastest production car in the world, with a fastest recorded speed of 413 km/h (257 mph). This speed was reportedly achieved during tests on September 13, 2007 in West Richland, Washington, United States and verified by Guinness World Records on October 9, 2007.

The Aero and the Shelby SuperCars company are the brainchildren of Jerod Shelby, who spent over seven years designing the car. Although the basic Aero model is no longer produced, the Ultimate Aero is still in production with an MSRP of around $654,400. SSC announced the production of the Ultimate Aero EV, an electrical version of the sports car. The released specifications include using 500 horsepower (373 kW) electric motor, with SSC also exploring the potential of using 2 engines in 2 or 4 wheel drive configuration. The SSC, once in production, will be the fastest electric car on the market. "I think we can do it faster, leaner and cleaner than any other manufacturer," claims the SSC founder, Jerod Shelby. SSC planned to produce its first prototype in February 2009, with production to begin as early as Q4 of 2009.

TESLA ROADSTER

The Tesla Roadster is an all-electric sports car produced by the electric car firm Tesla Motors and is the first car produced by the company. The Roadster can travel 244 miles (393 km) on a single charge of its lithium-ion battery pack, and can accelerate from 0–60 mph (0–97 km/h) in 3.9 seconds. An improved, Sport version of the Roadster was released in January, 2009 with adjustable dampers and a new hand-wound motor, capable of 0–60 mph (0–97 km/h) in 3.7 seconds. The Roadster's efficiency, as of September 2008, was reported as 120 mpgge (2.0 L/100 km). It uses 135 W·h/km (4.60 mi/kW·h) battery-to-wheel, and has an efficiency of 92% on average. The Roadster was developed with design help from Lotus Cars, who supplied the basic chassis development technology from the Lotus Elise. First unveiled to the public on 19 July 2006, series production of the car began on 17 March 2008. Tesla's "Signature One Hundred" initial set of fully equipped cars sold out by late August, 2006. Tesla Motors then began accepting reservation orders by September, 2006 for their 2008 models, with several payment options available to determine the 2008 delivery date of the vehicle. The second hundred had been reserved by October. As of January 15, 2008, all 650 Tesla Roadsters planned for model year 2008 had been reserved. As it was initially only available in the USA, where traffic stays to the right-hand side of the road (RHT), Roadsters are available only with the steering-wheel on the left-hand side (LHD). For 2009, Tesla plans to deliver 1500 cars. The price for the 2009 models has increased to US$109,000; options ranging from colors to audio to heavy duty cables can add another $10,000 By February 2009 Tesla had reached an agreement to open stores in Chicago, and was close to finalizing locations in Miami, New York, and Seattle.